GREAT

MOVIE

LINES

D0180455

FAWCETT COLUMBINE / NEW YORK

GREAT
MOVIE
LINES

EDITED BY
Dale Thomajan

A Fawcett Columbine Book
Published by Ballantine Books
Copyright © 1993 by Dale Thomajan

All rights reserved under International and Pan-
American Copyright Conventions. Published in the
United States by Ballantine Books, a division of
Random House, Inc., New York, and simultaneously
in Canada by Random House of Canada Limited,
Toronto.

Library of Congress Catalog Card Number: 92-97333
ISBN: 0-449-90802-x

Text design by Beth Tondreau Design / Mary A. Wirth

Manufactured in the United States of America
First Edition: July 1993
10 9 8 7 6 5 4 3 2

TO
PRESTON
STURGES

O ne of the things I love about movies is that nearly everyone in them can be counted on to say the right thing at the right time. Not once in my life do I recall anybody saying the right thing—the *exact* right thing—to me at the right time, or me saying it to anyone (though many's the time I thought of it later). It only happens in the movies.

The golden age of movie dialogue was the 1930s; performers in that decade were almost always saying terrific things to each other. (The rest of the time they were saying "*Gee*, you're swell.") It's kind of eerie to realize that these memorable lines were delivered before most of us were born—and that virtually all of the men and women who appeared in movies of the early '30s are now dead. Yet—thanks to repertory cinemas, television, videocassette transferal, and the film preservation crusade—these people are still alive to us. I was about to call them ghosts, but as they will continue to speak these same lines—the lines they first spoke before we were born—after we're gone, maybe it's we who are the ghosts.

What follows are 200 of the most eloquent, witty, moving, clever, silly, poetic, and outrageous things uttered on the screen since the advent of the talking picture. As you read these lines—which I have arranged in what I hope is a sequentially meaningful way—see if you can identify their contexts (revealed in the back of the book, beginning on page 201).

Without further ado then, allow me to conclude this introduction by invoking what is believed to be the most oft-spoken movie line of all time: "Let's get out of here."

D. T.

I only saw her for one second. She didn't see me at all, but I'll bet a month hasn't gone by since, that I haven't thought of that girl.

Man, she looked as if she'd just
been thrown off the
crummiest freight train
in the world.

I know I must look funny to you but maybe if you went to Mandrake Falls you'd look just as funny to us—only nobody'd laugh at you and make you feel ridiculous, 'cause that wouldn't be good manners.

won't be wronged. I won't be insulted. I won't be laid a hand on. I don't do these things to other people and I require the same from them.

That's one of the tragedies of this life—that the men who are most in need of a beating-up are always enormous.

f I want your opinion I'll beat it out of you.

Come and get one in the
yarbles, if you have any
yarbles, you eunuch jelly thou!

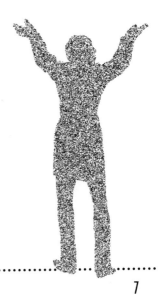

f I had choice of weapons with you, sir, I'd choose grammar.

Now, I am in no position to mention their names by name but I can tell you this—they are the kind of types that have been known to act very hotheaded in their day and age.

Ma'am, I sure like that name—
Clementine.

And this, this is, this is the most interesting thing about the whole thing—he said "What a coincidence. My name happens to *be* Harvey."

Honest, sensible, sober,
harmless Holly Martins.
Holly—what a silly name.

How many honest men you know? You take the sinners away from the saints, you're lucky to end up with Abraham Lincoln.

'm plain Abraham Lincoln. . . . If elected I shall be thankful. If not it'll be all the same.

I coulda been a contender.

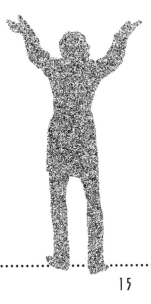

treated her like a pair of gloves.
When I was cold I called her up.

Look up, Hannah! Look up!

Keep watching the skies!

"Supernatural"—perhaps. "Baloney"—perhaps not. There are many things under the sun.

You know, the nice thing
about buying food for a man
is that you don't have to
laugh at his jokes.

There's a lot to be said for making people laugh. Did you know that's all some people have?

If we bring a little joy into your humdrum lives it makes us feel as though our hard work ain't been in vain fer nothing.

Aman works all his life in a glass factory, one day he feels like picking up a hammer.

I've been waiting all my life to fuck up like this.

....

I've been trying for three years to find out if it's possible to live what I think is a civilized life, a life that can't hurt any other life.

....

I t doesn't hurt any more—
now or ever again!

You made us in the House of Pain. You made us—*things*.

Get your state troopers out to my place. I got something trapped in my barn.

don't like the country. The
crickets make me nervous.

Was you ever bit by a dead bee?

I never dreamed that any mere physical experience could be so stimulating.

My experience I can give you in a nutshell and I didn't dream it in a dream either.

Last night I dreamt I went to Manderley again.

And it *seemed* real, it *seemed* like us, and it seemed like, well, our home—if not Arizona then a land not too far away, where all parents are strong and wise and capable, and all children are happy and beloved. I don't know. Maybe it was Utah.

You call this a happy family?
Why do we have to have
all these kids?

Listen to them—children of the night. What music they make.

Nobody handles Handel like you handle Handel!

Nobody loses all the time.

'm not a failure. I'm a success.
And so are you if you earn your
own living and pay your bills and
look the world in the eye.

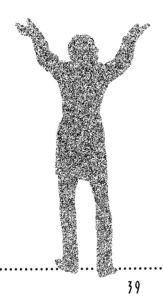

All I want is to enter my house justified.

W e're in Hell. We entered Hell.
When?

s he in Heaven? Is he in Hell?
That damned elusive Pimpernel.

What he did to Shakespeare we are doing now to Poland.

43

You have no idea what a long-legged gal can do without doing anything.

There are two kinds of people—those who don't do what they want to do so they write down in a diary about what they haven't done, and those who are too busy to write about it, because they're out doing it.

My diary's simply *full* of him.

Y ou caught him with sex but sex isn't the only thing in life and when it's gone you'll lose him— because then he'll want love and love is the one thing you don't know anything about and never will!

The psychiatrist asked me if I had a girl and I said no and he said, well, do I think that sex is dirty and I said it is if you're doing it right.

Mr. Allen, this may come as a shock to you but there are some men who don't end every sentence with a proposition.

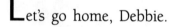
Let's go home, Debbie.

Thank you, but I always go home with the man who brought me.

Aw, you can be had.

Aw, I wouldn't go for that dame if she was the last woman on earth—and I just got out of the Navy.

It's time to get out. We have to touch Indians. We have to see the mountains and the prairies and the whole rest of that song!

You know what I think? I think that—we're all in our private traps, clamped in them, and none of us can ever get out.

She shall be shut up in the house where they keep the mad. I, Gogol, will do that. *She* shall be shut up when it's *I* who am mad.

We all go a little mad
sometimes.

Oh, please, Mother—tell me all about the crazy and idiotic things you did when you were my age.

Maybe if a man *looks* ugly he does ugly things.

If she cut off her head she'd be very pretty.

You were extremely attractive . . . but you were a little worse, or better, for wine—and there are rules about that.

Oh, champagne—I love it! It tastes like your foot's asleep.

Popeye, you still picking your feet in Poughkeepsie?

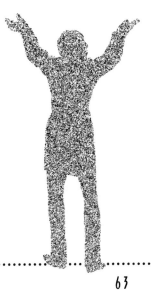

When a cop dies they don't list
it as heart failure—just
Charley horse of the chest.

I'm Mimi. I'm dying.

What are you going to do, kill me? Everybody dies.

When it comes to dying for your country, it's better not to die at all.

Well, that's the war for you—
always hard on women.
Either they take your men away
and never send them back a-tall or
they send them back unexpectedly
just to embarrass you.

Never again will I allow women
to wear my dresses!

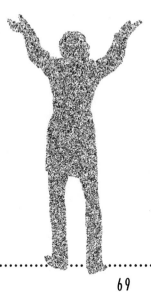

How old is a woman like you?

Old age. It's the only disease, Mr. Thompson, that you don't look forward to being cured of.

Live fast. Die young. Have a good-looking corpse.

She ate a poisoned cheese sandwich and turned up her toes.

The big ones eat the little ones up here.

He rode a man and a little person down in the streets of Winslow—maybe it was a child.

It's a hard world for little things.

'm sicka hearing about men that do the little things. Give me a guy that does a big thing once in a while, like paying a month's rent.

You know, you don't have to act with me, Steve. You don't have to say anything and you don't have to do anything. Not a thing. Oh, maybe just whistle.

Maybe there ain't no sin and there ain't no virtue. It's just what people does.

What rotten Sins I've got
working for me. I suppose
it's the wages.

Do you know that she makes $45 a week and sends her mother a hundred of it?

Women are weak and men are strong. My mother wasted a lifetime of strength trying to prove that.

Power—it's come to a common, vulgar fellow and it's driven me *wild*.

A pushing sort of girl, a very
pushing little person.

f she's a girl, then I don't know
what my sister is.

M oja sestra. Moja sestra?

Do you speak Canadian at all?

I've dug in Alaska and Canada and Colorado ... all over the world practically. Yeah, I know what gold does to men's souls.

know the world's been shaved by
a drunken barber.

I know exactly how you feel, my dear. The morning after always does look grim if you happen to be wearing last night's dress.

know you want me to tear my clothes off so's you can look your fifty cents' worth. Fifty cents for the privilege of staring at a girl the way your wives won't let you!

That was really embarrassing.
Thank you for including me.

Oh, I'm sorry. I didn't realize I was disturbing you. You see, every once in a while I suddenly find myself—dancing.

"Sorry" don't get it done, Dude.

've done my time with one cold-blooded bastard. I'm not looking for another.

Rick Von Sloneker is tall, rich, good-looking, stupid, dishonest, conceited, a bully, liar, drunk, and thief, an egomaniac, and probably psychotic—in short, highly attractive to women.

You see, Hopsie, you don't know very much about girls. The best ones aren't as good as you probably think they are, and the bad ones aren't as bad— not nearly as bad.

I don't suppose any man has ever understood any woman since the beginning of things. You don't understand our imaginations— how wild our imaginations can be.

When women go wrong, men go right after them.

A nd she says "You and who else?" And I says "Oh, yeah?" And she says "Yeah is right." So I says "You and me both." She says "That goes double for me." I says "Oh, yeah?"

S he only said no once and then
she didn't hear the question.

What Jefferson was saying was "Hey! you know, we left this England place 'cause it was *bogus*, so if we don't get some cool rules ourselves—*pronto*—we'll just be bogus too."

To a new world of gods and monsters.

drink a la most beautiful
femme de la champ. Elle knows
who elle is.

Honest to goodness, every time you'd turn 'round that Frenchman was a-grabbing for your hand and kissing until he'd like to pull the skin off.

That's good. You've stopped kissing me like I was your auntie.

know a guy married the same dame three times, then turned around and married her aunt.

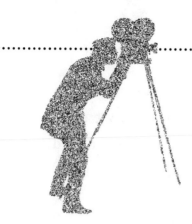

been around that trashy behavior
all my life.

’ll be around in the dark. I'll be everywhere—wherever you can look.

Oh, Beulah . . . peel me a grape.

You can serve tea and screw,
Arlington.

The pellet with the poison's in the vessel with the pestle. The chalice from the palace has the brew that is true.

Do I know them? I positively swill in their ale.

H ere's looking at you, kid.

Life's a queer little man, kiddie.

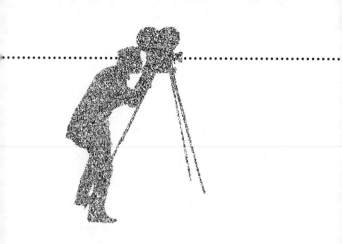

Yes, smaller than the smallest, I meant something too. To God there is no zero. I still exist.

He used to be a big shot.

M other of Mercy, is this the end
of Rico?

'm talking about you, you
ridiculous old-fashioned jug-
eared lopsided Little Caesar.

If you want to call me that, smile.

If you want to find an outlaw,
you call an outlaw. If you want
to find a Dunkin' Donuts,
call a cop.

Badges? We ain't got no badges. We don't need no badges. *I don't have to show you any stinkin' badges!*

Y ou're not too smart—are you? I
like that in a man.

You know, the first man that can think up a good explanation how he can be in love with his wife *and* another woman is going to win that prize they're always giving out in Sweden.

B aby, you're the key to my ignition.

$\int$ ome day a car will stop to pick
me up that I never thumbed.

Love has got to stop some place short of suicide.

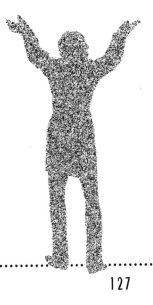

You realize that suicide is a criminal offense. In less enlightened times they'd have hung you for it.

In Italy for thirty years under the Borgias they had warfare, terror, murder, and bloodshed, but they produced Michelangelo, Leonardo da Vinci, and the Renaissance. In Switzerland they had brotherly love—they had five hundred years of democracy and peace, and what did that produce?
The cuckoo clock.

Ninotchka, it's midnight. One half of Paris is making love to the other half.

can't believe it. Right here where we *live*. Right here in St. Louis.

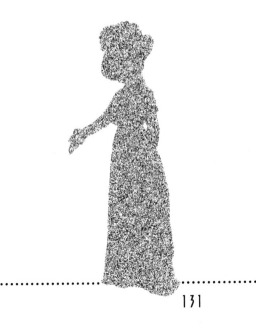

Jake, we don't want to conquer
the world. We only want to
live in it.

M ade it, Ma. Top of the world!

f we don't make that bus stop—
remember me.

That's all I'm trying to do with this money—help the fellas who can't make the hill on high.

'm working on my first million—
and you're still working on eight
seconds.

Bick, you should have shot that fella a long time ago. Now he's too rich to kill.

Shooting's what I'm good at.
It's what I want to do when
I grow up.

What I really want to do with my life, what I want to do for a living—I want to be with your daughter. I'm good at it.

Bend down, Papa ... My cup runneth over.

f Pa just hangs on to that black colt, everything's going to be OK.

I didn't squawk about the steak, dear. I merely said I didn't see that old horse that used to be tethered outside here.

'll give you a dollar if you eat this collie.

"Joe Bob's Fine Foods—Eat Here or I'll Kill You."

t's the sort of place where you
have to wear a shirt.

That's a nice outfit but you'd better add to it before you go to church.

don't go to church. Kneeling
bags my nylons.

Evidently you're a very amusing person.

One of the finest women ever
walked the streets.

Outside, Countess. As long as they've got sidewalks, you've got a job.

It took more than one man
to change my name
to Shanghai Lily.

I guess it was easier for her to change her name than for her whole family to change theirs.

Anne Schuyler's in the Blue Book. You're not even in the phone book.

It's lucky for you, sir, I'm not a vindictive person. You've just done me a terrible injustice.

John, every day you act worse
but today you're acting like
tomorrow.

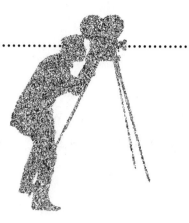

always liked gentle people. Me? I'm hard—hard and tough. I got no use for hard people.

You're one of those self-indulgent males who thinks about nothing but his clothes, his car, himself. Bet you do push-ups every morning just to keep your belly hard.

From now on you're the only
man in the world that my door
is closed to.

Frankly, my dear, I don't give a damn.

159

When I get back to my room
you're the only thing I want
to find missing.

Crime is only a left-handed
form of human endeavor.

When teenagers complain that they want to be treated like human beings it's usually because they *are* being treated like human beings.

Mom, Dad, this is Judy.
She's my friend.

And oh, Auntie Em, there's *no* place like home.

Harry, Harry, look! The mechanical man is crying!

Harry's an artist without an art.

He's whittling on a piece of wood. I got a feeling when he stops whittling—something's gonna happen.

There's something in the
atmosphere that makes
everything seem exaggerated.

How would you like to go over the park with me and help me tramp down all the flowers?

Oh, Jerry, don't let's ask for the moon. We have the stars.

You want the moon? . . . Hey, that's a pretty good idea—I'll give you the moon, Mary.

I want to be alone.

It wasn't the first time I went to bed with a guy and woke up with a note.

$\int$ ome kind of fun lasts longer than others, if you get what I mean.

In the words of Marcel Proust—
and this applies to any woman
in the world—if you can stay up
and listen with a fair degree of
attention to whatever garbage, no

matter how
stupid it is,
that they're
coming out with 'til
ten minutes past four
in the morning,
you're in.

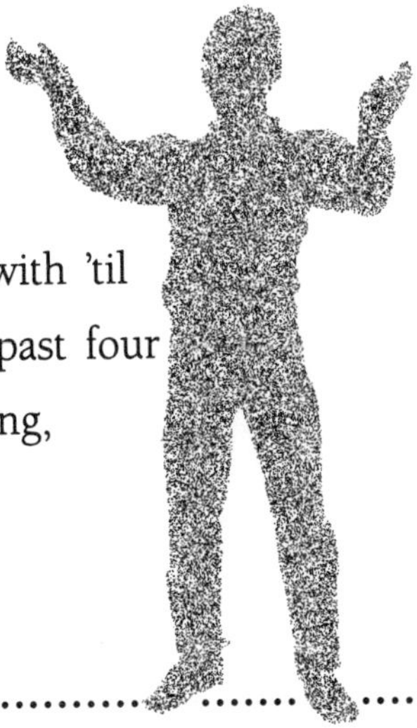

A guy'll listen to anything if he thinks it's foreplay.

We didn't need dialogue. We had *faces*.

call him the boy with the ice
cream face.

This chick is *toast*.

What are you going to do—
shoot something for
breakfast?

My life has been one glorious hunt. It would be impossible for me to tell you how many animals I have killed.

One morning I shot an
elephant in my pajamas.
How he got in my pajamas
I don't know.

From the looks of those ears she's gonna fly before she'll walk.

I told you she was different.

$\int$he tried to sit on my lap while I was standing up.

t all sounds so fascinatin'
and uncouth.

Bull, you ain't no oil paintin'
but you're a fascinatin'
monster.

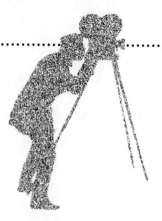

Oh, no, it wasn't the airplanes—it was beauty killed the beast.

That's funny ... That plane's dusting crops where there ain't no crops.

My room, bumpkin.
I'm pooped.

Oh, shut up, you dern little cuss, you little fool. You ain't had that there coat and them pants on for six months, yet you talk as if you was *George* Washington.

'm not trying to be a hero!
I'm fighting the dragon!

Remember, you're fighting for this woman's honor, which is probably more than she ever did.

It'd be a terrific innovation if you could get your mind to stretch a little further than the next wisecrack.

You know, don't you, that you and Tex are all I've got left in the world and I'd cut my heart out for you. Please don't be mad at me.

With all my heart I still love
the man I killed.

Yes, I killed him. I killed him for money and for a woman. Well, I didn't get the money and I didn't get the woman.

Maybe I'll live so long that I'll forget her. Maybe I'll die trying.

I was born when she kissed me. I died when she left me. I lived a few weeks while she loved me.

Rosebud.

1. Everett Sloane in *Citizen Kane*, 1941
2. Tom Neal about Ann Savage in *Detour*, 1945
3. Gary Cooper to a bunch of city slickers in *Mr. Deeds Goes to Town*, 1936
4. John Wayne in *The Shootist*, 1976
5. Rudy Vallee in *The Palm Beach Story*, 1942
6. Tough cop Chuck Norris to a heckling punk in *Code of Silence*, 1985
7. Malcolm McDowell to a rival gang leader in *A Clockwork Orange*, 1971
8. Halliwell Hobbes to Ned Sparks in *Lady for a Day*, 1933
9. Spencer Tracy in *Pat and Mike*, 1952
10. Henry Fonda to Cathy Downs in *My Darling Clementine*, 1946
11. James Stewart about an invisible

rabbit he has befriended in *Harvey*,
1950

12. (Alida) Valli to Joseph Cotten (Holly
    Martins) in *The Third Man*, 1949
13. Paul Newman to Melvyn Douglas in
    Hud, 1963
14. Henry Fonda in *Young Mr. Lincoln*,
    1939
15. Ex-boxer Marlon Brando in *On the
    Waterfront*, 1954
16. Cornel Wilde about Helene Stanton
    in *The Big Combo*, 1955
17. Charles Chaplin to Paulette Goddard
    (and the world) in *The Great Dictator*,
    1940
18. Douglas Spencer in *The Thing from
    Another World*, 1951
19. Bela Lugosi to a skeptical David
    Manners in *The Black Cat*, 1934
20. Veronica Lake to Joel McCrea in
    Sullivan's Travels, 1941
21. Movie comedy director Joel McCrea
    in *Sullivan's Travels*, 1941

22. Silent movie star Jean Hagen to her public in *Singin' in the Rain*, 1952

23. Harold Lloyd in *The Sin of Harold Diddlebock*, 1947

24. Michael Moriarty in *Who'll Stop the Rain?*, 1978

25. James Cagney in *The Time of Your Life*, 1948

26. Joel McCrea as W. T. G. Morton, the discoverer of anesthesia, in *The Great Moment*, 1944

27. Bela Lugosi to Charles Laughton in *Island of Lost Souls*, 1933

28. Lillian Gish phoning for help with Robert Mitchum in *The Night of the Hunter*, 1955

29. Marlon Brando in *On the Waterfront*, 1954

30. Walter Brennan in *To Have and Have Not*, 1945

31. Katharine Hepburn to Humphrey Bogart after shooting the rapids with him in *The African Queen*, 1951

Jack Benny's acting talent in *To Be or Not to Be*, 1942

44. Claudette Colbert in *The Palm Beach Story*, 1942

45. Charles Coburn in *The More the Merrier*, 1943

46. Jeanne Crain about her French teacher in *Margie*, 1946

47. Leila Hyams to Jean Harlow about Chester Morris in *Red-Headed Woman*, 1932

48. Woody Allen in *Take the Money and Run*, 1969

49. Doris Day to Rock Hudson in *Pillow Talk*, 1959

50. John Wayne to Natalie Wood in *The Searchers*, 1956

51. Gloria Grahame to Humphrey Bogart in *In a Lonely Place*, 1950

52. Mae West to Cary Grant in *She Done Him Wrong*, 1933

53. James Cagney in *Taxi!*, 1932

77. Mary Phillips in *Mannequin*, 1937
78. Lauren Bacall to Humphrey Bogart in *To Have and Have Not*, 1945
79. John Carradine in *The Grapes of Wrath*, 1940
80. Peter Cook as the Devil in *Bedazzled*, 1967
81. Ginger Rogers in *42nd Street*, 1933
82. Joan Crawford in *Mannequin*, 1937
83. Roland Young as *The Man Who Could Work Miracles*, 1937
84. Hedda Hopper about Katharine Hepburn in *Alice Adams*, 1935
85. Newsboy Barry Gordon about Jayne Mansfield in *The Girl Can't Help It*, 1956
86. Elizabeth Russell recognizing a kindred spirit in Simone Simon in *Cat People*, 1943
87. North Dallas Bulls executive Dabney Coleman to fading football star Nick Nolte in *North Dallas Forty*, 1979

88. Walter Huston in *The Treasure of the Sierra Madre*, 1948

89. Walter Brennan in *Meet John Doe*, 1941

90. Ina Claire to Greta Garbo in *Ninotchka*, 1939

91. Maureen O'Hara to a burlesque show audience in *Dance, Girl, Dance*, 1940

92. Taylor Nichols to Edward Clements in *Metropolitan*, 1990

93. Fred Astaire to Ginger Rogers in *Top Hat*, 1935

94. John Wayne to Dean Martin in *Rio Bravo*, 1959

95. Patricia Neal to Paul Newman in *Hud*, 1963

96. Christopher Eigeman about Will Kempe in *Metropolitan*, 1990

97. Barbara Stanwyck to Henry Fonda in *The Lady Eve*, 1941

98. Margaretta Scott to Raymond Massey in *Things to Come*, 1936

99. Mae West in *She Done Him Wrong*, 1933

100. Frank C. Moran to Harry Rosenthal in *The Great McGinty*, 1940

101. George E. Stone about Ginger Rogers ("Anytime Annie") in *42nd Street*, 1933

102. Sean Penn paraphrasing American history in *Fast Times at Ridgemont High*, 1982

103. Ernest Thesiger raising a toast in *The Bride of Frankenstein*, 1935

104. Peter Lawford to Patricia Marshall in *Good News*, 1947

105. Maude Eburne in *Among the Living*, 1941

106. Clare Grogan to Gordon John Sinclair in *Gregory's Girl*, 1981

107. William Demarest in *The Lady Eve*, 1941

108. Ben Johnson in *The Last Picture Show*, 1971

109. Henry Fonda bidding his mother

good-bye in *The Grapes of Wrath*, 1940

110. Mae West to her maid in *I'm No Angel*, 1933

111. James Cagney to his servant in *Jimmy the Gent*, 1934

112. Mildred Natwick to Danny Kaye in *The Court Jester*, 1956

113. Eric Blore about the Pike Ale family in *The Lady Eve*, 1941

114. Humphrey Bogart to Ingrid Bergman in *Casablanca*, 1942

115. Wendell Corey to Jack Palance in *The Big Knife*, 1955

116. Grant Williams as *The Incredible Shrinking Man*, 1957

117. Gladys George's epitaph for James Cagney in *The Roaring Twenties*, 1939

118. Edward G. Robinson's dying words in *Little Caesar*, 1931

119. Janet Leigh to Akim Tamiroff in *Touch of Evil*, 1958

120. Gary Cooper to Walter Huston in *The Virginian*, 1929

121. Randall "Tex" Cobb in *Raising Arizona*, 1987

122. Alfonso Bedoya to Humphrey Bogart in *The Treasure of the Sierra Madre*, 1948

123. Kathleen Turner to William Hurt in *Body Heat*, 1981

124. Mary Cecil in *The Women*, 1939

125. Charlotte Greenwood to Eddie Cantor in *Palmy Days*, 1931

126. Fugitive Tom Neal in *Detour*, 1945

127. Walter Huston to the wife he's leaving in *Dodsworth*, 1936

128. Peter Cook to Dudley Moore in *Bedazzled*, 1967

129. Orson Welles in *The Third Man*, 1949

130. Melvyn Douglas to Greta Garbo in *Ninotchka*, 1939

131. Judy Garland in *Meet Me in St. Louis*, 1944

132. Gertrude Berg to her husband, Philip Loeb, in *Molly*, 1950

133. James Cagney, atop an oil tanker, about to be blown to Hell in *White Heat*, 1949

134. Cloris Leachman to Ralph Meeker in *Kiss Me Deadly*, 1955

135. Gary Cooper in *Mr. Deeds Goes to Town*, 1936

136. Joe Don Baker to his brother, rodeo cowboy Steve McQueen, in *Junior Bonner*, 1972

137. Chill Wills to Rock Hudson about James Dean in *Giant*, 1956

138. Rusty (Russ) Tamblyn in *Gun Crazy*, 1950

139. John Cusack to Ione Skye's father in *Say Anything*, 1989

140. Peggy Ann Garner to James Dunn in *A Tree Grows in Brooklyn*, 1945

141. Sterling Hayden's dying words in *The Asphalt Jungle*, 1950

142. W. C. Fields to his waitress in *Never Give a Sucker an Even Break*, 1941

143. Martin Sheen's first line in *Badlands*, 1973

144. Nick Nolte suggesting a slogan for Bo Svenson's restaurant in *North Dallas Forty*, 1979

145. Claire Trevor inviting Dick Powell out in *Murder, My Sweet*, 1945

146. Cornel Wilde to Ida Lupino in *Road House*, 1948

147. Jan Sterling to Kirk Douglas in *Ace in the Hole*, 1951

148. Katharine Hepburn to Ginger Rogers in *Stage Door*, 1937

149. Mae West about herself in *She Done Him Wrong*, 1933

150. Joan Blondell to Claire Dodd in *Footlight Parade*, 1933

151. Marlene Dietrich in *Shanghai Express*, 1932

152. Irene Dunne about Joyce Compton in *The Awful Truth*, 1937

Wood to his parents in *Rebel Without a Cause*, 1955

164. Judy Garland in *The Wizard of Oz*, 1939

165. Helen Gibson to her escort about Wally Cassell in *City That Never Sleeps*, 1953

166. Hugh Marlowe about Richard Widmark in *Night and the City*, 1950

167. Jason Robards, Jr., about Charles Bronson in *Once Upon a Time in the West*, 1969

168. David Farrar in *Black Narcissus*, 1947

169. Spencer Tracy to Joan Bennett in *Me and My Gal*, 1932

170. Bette Davis to Paul Henreid in *Now, Voyager*, 1942

171. James Stewart courting Donna Reed in *It's a Wonderful Life*, 1946

172. Greta Garbo in *Grand Hotel*, 1932

173. Susan Sarandon in *Bull Durham*, 1988

174. Betty Hutton broaching her

pregnancy to Eddie Bracken in *The Miracle of Morgan's Creek*, 1944

175. Peter Cook to Dudley Moore in *Bedazzled*, 1967

176. Susan Sarandon in *Bull Durham*, 1988

177. Silent movie star Gloria Swanson in *Sunset Boulevard*, 1950

178. Emile Meyer about Tony Curtis in *Sweet Smell of Success*, 1957

179. Bill Murray right before zapping an Amazonian diety with his laser gun in *Ghostbusters*, 1984

180. Marie Windsor to Charles McGraw in *The Narrow Margin*, 1952

181. Leslie Banks in *The Most Dangerous Game*, 1932

182. Groucho Marx in *Animal Crackers*, 1930

183. Lawrence Tierney commenting on a snapshot of a gas station attendant's baby daughter in *The Devil Thumbs a Ride*, 1947

184. Richard Widmark's dying words to Cornel Wilde after being shot by Ida Lupino in *Road House*, 1948

185. Humphrey Bogart about Martha Vickers in *The Big Sleep*, 1946

186. Carroll Baker in *Giant*, 1956

187. Mae West to Victor McLaglen in *Klondike Annie*, 1936

188. Robert Armstrong in *King Kong*, 1933

189. Andy Albin to Cary Grant in *North by Northwest*, 1959

190. Daffy Duck to Elmer Fudd in *The Scarlet Pumpernickel*, 1950

191. John Dierkes to Bill Mauldin in *The Red Badge of Courage*, 1951

192. Ed Harris in *Knightriders*, 1981

193. Groucho Marx to his brethren regarding Margaret Dumont in *Duck Soup*, 1933

194. Katharine Hepburn to Eve Arden in *Stage Door*, 1937

195. James Cagney to Pat O'Brien in *Ceiling Zero*, 1936

ACKNOWLEDGMENTS

"My mother thanks you. My father thanks you. My sister thanks you. And I thank you."*

Timothy Hamilton
Thelma Adjano
Arto DeMirjian, Jr.
Richard T. Jameson
Mal Ethan Joad
Donald Phelps
Donald Silva
G. J. Rigopoulos
Margo Smith
Mary South of Ballantine Books

*James Cagney in *Yankee Doodle Dandy*